Birthing
PURPOSE

Against

All

Odds

Library of Congress Cataloging-in-Publication Data
Beard, Daphne.
Birthing Purpose Against All Odds / Daphne Beard. – 1st ed.
ISBN 978-0999147603
1. Religion / Christian Life / Personal Growth

First Edition.
Printed in the United States of America
2017910129

I dedicate this book to...

...the wise and witty woman of God who told the five-year-old me, "You can do anything you set your mind on doing."

...a true servant who touched the lives of tens of thousands over the course of her life by sheltering broken women, feeding homeless families and caring for total strangers.

...a no-nonsense woman who spoke her mind and stood for holiness.

...a woman who publically and privately loved Jesus.

...a woman who gave all she had for those she loved.

...a woman who left a legacy of love in action by imparting in the lives of so many, including my own.

...a woman who allowed me to sit at her feet and receive wisdom.

...a woman who exemplified unwavering integrity, unrestricted honesty and unconditional love.

In memory of my beloved grandmother, my intercessory prayer warrior, the late and great, "99.9-percent perfect" **Mary Rose Battle**, a woman who fearlessly birthed purpose with grace and tenacity!

Contents

Preface

First and foremost, I must make clear that little to nothing in this book is the result of human intuition but rather the result of obedience to God through fasting and prayer. As God gave me the words for this book, the intensity of spiritual warfare I experienced increased. In fact, the intensity seemed relentless, which assured me that you, the reader, have not simply opened any ordinary book. You have uncovered a weapon of war—one that the Enemy does not want you to finish because he knows the tools given here by the Holy Spirit will catapult you into God's purpose for your life. I fought long and hard to finish this book, but my fight was not for me alone; my battle was also for you.

My goal is to awaken the innate purpose of God in your life by challenging your existing awareness of who you are with the truth of who God wants you to be. This book is not for those who have already "arrived"; rather, it is for those who are never satisfied with where they are, who they are and whose hearts often beat to the drum of "I know there's more." Here is the disclaimer: fulfilling this desire will not be easy, but I promise, it is worth it. You will "consider your ways" (Haggai 1:5-7) and discover tools that will empower you to overcome internal and external obstacles that prevent you from walking confidently into the purpose of God for your life.

As you read, it would behoove you to be aware of resistance that rises up within you. It is probable in such moments that God is speaking directly to the part of you that resists "the more" of God. By nature, we are creatures of habit and what does not fit into our habitual practices is often resisted. However, the truth of the matter is in order to unlock the "more" of God's purpose, you must possess the willingness to become uncomfortable, the maturity to stop blaming others, the courage to confront your own idiosyncrasies and the resilience to endure the process.

Be assured, this is not another self-help book on how to be all you can be; it is a manual on what you will encounter while birthing purpose and what you will need to ensure it lives against all odds. Proverbs 20:18 says, "*Every* purpose is established by counsel: and with good advice make war." The word *purpose* in this scripture is interpreted in the original Greek form as *machashabah* which means "a work or a plan." Therefore, every work that God calls us to do must have a sturdy foundation built on Godly instruction that will survive opposition. Birthing purpose or the process of giving life to divine intention is anything but a walk in the park. It is a real battle, a real fight. Nonetheless, like a jubilant first-time mother who takes the first look into the face of her newborn baby, you too will declare, "It was all worth it!"

My prayer is that your heart will respond with a resounding "Yes!" to receive and utilize the tools God has placed in this book to better equip you to produce the purpose of God in your life. I wholeheartedly believe that after receiving the truths packed into this book, your life will never ever be the same! To God be the glory!

Introduction

Five years ago, God told me to write this book, but I allowed the cares of life to take precedence over what God said. Despite the fact that He gave me the chapter titles, content and experience to include in this book, I allowed subtle distractions such as furthering my education and pursing my career draw me away from the task He had given me. In August of 2015, I felt such urgency in my spirit to complete this project that I knew then this was more than a book. God had given me an assignment—one that I had no idea how I would ever complete because I was inundated with school, work, ministry and life obligations. Two months later, God sent a prophet to me who confirmed, "The Lord said write the book." Once the Lord made public what was once private between He and I, I knew He had something that He wanted to say.

After the prophetic word was released, I started writing again. A mere two months later, I learned that I needed emergency surgery, which I will address in the chapters to come. This unfortunate reality caused me to place this manuscript on the back burner yet again. About six months after the eye surgery, I had a gall bladder attack that also required immediate surgery. I was literally folded in half, unable to stand or take normal breaths because of the intensity of the pain. As I suffered in that hospital bed, it dawned on me that my physical body was manifesting what was happening spiritually. My physical body was under attack a spiritual attack.

At that point, I began to use my weapons (See 2 Corinthians 10:4) and call on the name of Jesus. After prayer, I declined the surgery in spite of what the doctors recommended. I knew I had to trust God with my health. Certainly, I am not advising any person under physician care to ignore the doctors' orders; rather, I am sharing my story, which I believe was the result of divine instruction. After prayer, I clearly understood that I had to let Hell know I would not be stopped. God had given me an opportunity to stand firm on the Word of

God and believe that with His stripes we were healed (Isaiah 53:5). Preaching His Word is not enough; I had to apply it in my daily life. I had to believe that Jesus, the One who shed His blood for me, would heal and keep me against all odds Thanks be to God, that is exactly what He did—no more pain or additional attacks!

Approximately four months later, I was running late to a presentation at my job, and in my haste to get out of the door, I fell down one step. This fall left me with a sprained right ankle, two weeks on crutches, a boot that caused my hip to become out of alignment, an ankle brace and finally three months of physical therapy. And last, but not least, I was unable to drive, work or wear the heels I wanted to wear! Trust me, the ban on heels was a major problem in my life!

I want you to understand something about birthing purpose: it is not easy. Purpose is not handed to anyone on a silver platter. A person must suffer for, cry over, bleed for, sweat over and pray immensely that God would strengthen them in the process. The fact that you are holding this book should prove to you that nothing and nobody can stop the purpose of God for your life. After all of the attacks I endured (many of which I have not included in this book), I am thankful for each one. If I had not suffered through them, I would not have been able to share how to survive them. I want you to know this book was birthed out of my pain and suffering and is the result of many shed tears. By the end of this book, you will know that although we sow in tears, we will reap in joy (Psalm 126:5). Join me as we go on this journey together. I can promise you, if God could birth purpose through me against

all odds, He can do the same for you!

CHAPTER ONE

Mirror Moment

Pushing yourself to the limit has consequences. Going above and beyond has repercussions. During the summer of 2014, I decided to go after my dream of becoming a professional hospital chaplain. I researched, applied, interviewed and was selected to be a chaplain intern in a full-time clinical pastoral education (CPE) program. CPE is an interfaith curriculum that merges priest, pastors, ministers, imams and laypersons of various faiths together in a classroom setting to learn pastoral care skills needed for hospital ministry. Students are taught via didactics, textbooks, class work and homework. The program included a great deal of self-analysis of how one responded internally to what happened externally. Our group learned to process difficult emotions pertaining to past, present and future life events that led to increased self-awareness. The hope was the more self-awareness a chaplain gained, the more support he or she could provide to patients.

Sounds like an interesting journey that leads to something great, right? After all, the program offered the tools needed to answer that age-old question: "Who am I?" Without a doubt, CPE turned me inside out and caused me to face pains, failures, losses and disappointments that I wanted to keep somewhere in the closet behind the skeletons. I had no choice but to confront bitter heartbreaks, devastating deaths of loved ones, my own need to fix what is out of my control and other character flaws that I had chalked up to "personality." Side bar: the very thing that we consider to be a part of our personality (bad attitude, controlling ways, angry outburst, selfishness, greed, etc.) could be our own resistance to change for the better.

Now back to our regularly scheduled program... I learned more about myself in this year and a summer-long program than I had in my entire life. I felt stretched as a chaplain, a minister and overall, as a human being. However, the training was anything but easy. Little did I know that CPE would be much more intense than I had anticipated. Every week was a repetition of 20+

clinical hours in the hospital, 2-page written assignments, biweekly 5 to 7 page verbatim presentations, book reports, research projects and more.

Not only was the CPE workload intense, but I was also enrolled as a full-time online graduate student at Liberty University, studying to obtain my Master of Divinity in Chaplaincy. Attaining that goal meant even more papers, timed exams, projects, tons of reading and a nearly insurmountable amount of homework. Not to mention that I had commitments to family, ministry and all other life obligations—except social life, which was fairly nonexistent. Some nights I would not go to bed until 3:00 or 4:00 a.m. because I had to finish a paper that was due the following morning at 8:00 a.m.

At some point of reading through all of that, you likely rolled your eyes, shook your head or even thought "She must be crazy." Well, I would not argue you on that assessment. Choosing to commit to not one extremely demanding obligation, but two simultaneously, was anything but rational. Not only was my choice seemingly irrational, it was also physically taxing. I found myself in a constant state of stress coupled with anxiety that resulted in a terrible acne breakout on my forehead.

I had never before had an acne breakout— not even during puberty. Consequently, I had no idea how to treat the issue. I agonized and wondered how in the world this 25 year old could clear up a teenager's problem! Internet, that's how! I researched and purchased tons of over-the-counter treatments—to no avail. Most of the products were either too strong, dried out my skin or resulted in further spreading the acne. Next, I became desperate and decided I would try to squeeze, poke, prod, prick, and pop them, which of course, left ugly, dark marks on my face. At this point, I could not bear to look at myself in the mirror because I was no longer the woman I once knew. I tried to hide behind makeup, which led to even more severely irritated skin and additional breakouts. I resorted to using all-natural face washes and organic smoothies that were supposed to clear up the breakouts. I experienced some temporary relief that, unfortunately, did not last. I was fit to be tied. Done with it all. I did what I most likely should have done from the beginning (there is a message here that I will address later)—I anointed my face and cried out to God, asking Him to heal my face.

I was tired of having to filter my pictures on social media because of the embarrassing breakouts that now marred my once "secured" beauty. Me, insecure? Who ever heard of such a thing? Well, what I have shared is exactly where I was with this horrible breakout—totally insecure.

I cried, prayed, cried, prayed some more and suddenly while I was crying out to God, He led me to look in the mirror hanging behind my bedroom door. As I looked at my reflection, I heard God say, "What do you see?"

I replied, "Pimples here, dark spots there, a scar here."

Then He said, "You have named everything that is wrong with you and not one attribute that is right. What about your eyes? They are the eyes of a

18

woman who has seen so much bad but still looks for the good. What about your smile? Yours is the smile of a survivor who, despite every loss, still came out victorious. You must look beneath the blemishes and see the beauty. You are fearfully and wonderfully made. Now repeat it."

As I looked at myself in the mirror that day, with tears still rolling down my cheeks, I began to repeat, "I am fearfully and wonderfully made" until I believed it. I began to shout and declare it until I could look in that mirror and smile at the woman looking back. In that mirror moment, I realized I had a depth to me that could not be seen at a shallow level of observation. I had finally made it to the place where God wanted me to be from the beginning—a place where I could hear His voice louder than my own. My own voice was being manipulated by what I saw rather than what God saw.

How many times have you spoken ill of yourself out of your own mouth? How many times have you spoken directly against who God says you are? The point is, God wanted me to get to this place from the very beginning. However, rather than seeking Him, I immediately looked at what was within my power and what had worked for others to find a solution. How many times have you taken matters into your own hands and not consulted God?

When a problem arises, why is prayer seemingly the final option? Why is prayer not a believer's first line of defense? The message I learned and want to share is that God allowed me to have this breakout so He could show me where my trust really was—in the Internet (representing human knowledge) and in myself (representing my own ability.) In other words, I trusted in people and I trusted in me, but where was my trust in Him?

No doubt, like me, you also place great expectations on people and have confidence in yourself, but where is your trust in God? Lest we detach ourselves from what this world can offer us and our skill to obtain that which we desire, we will never walk into the purpose God intended for our lives.

Today is your day to get real with you. I want to invite you to the mirror. Seriously, go find the nearest mirror in your house, car, workplace, library or wherever you are reading this book. For those who are without a mirror, skip this section and come back to it once a mirror is nearby. I promise you won't regret it. To those who are in search of a mirror, I will give you some time. Do not miss this opportunity to grow. You owe it to yourself to take advantage of this mirror moment. This activity will show you something you may have otherwise never noticed. Okay, you should have a mirror by now. Let's begin.

Look in the mirror.
What was the first thing you noticed about yourself? _____
What did you notice about it?

_____

_____

Stare at yourself for 30 seconds. Yes, stare while allowing various thoughts to gallivant through your mind. Which thought do you recall the most?

_____

_____

_____

_____

What does that thought tell you about you?

_____

_____

_____

_____

Now let's discuss your mirror moment.

Pat, Covered, Morgan & Tim

A. If you answered, "My eyebrows need to be waxed," "There's sleep in my eye," "My lips are chapped," etc., you fall into the **"PAT"** category. Continue to letter **A**.

B. If you answered, "These lashes are giving me life," "This piercing is fire," "This hat is chic ," etc., you fall into the **"COVERED"** category. Continue to letter **B**.

23

C. If you answered, "My skin is glowing," "My eyes are bright," "My lips are perfect," etc., you fall into the "**MORGAN**" category. Continue to letter **C**.

D. If you answered, "Where are we going with this?" "Do I really need a mirror for this?" or "I need to figure out what I'm preparing for dinner," etc., then you fall into the "**TIM**" category. Continue to letter **D**.

A. PAT

"**PAT**" is one whose own perception is "Potentially A Threat." Pats tend to notice errors or problems with themselves that result in the inability to acknowledge the good. This tendency is often rooted in the need to be in control. Pats can overreact to situations over which they have no control. They talk themselves out of the greatest of ideas, including divine ideas because even in a God-inspired idea, Pats find a flaw. This need to find flaws often stems from insecurity, and prevents Pats from ever experiencing true peace within. Finding flaws also stops them from noticing progress. Their issue is not being overly cautious, but overly critical. Their perception is a potential threat to the purpose of God being fulfilled. In order to birth purpose, Pats should become more constructive and less condescending in assessing personal imperfections.

If you are a Pat, there is no need to be upset, bent out of shape or even disappointed—own it. God has been able to use billions of Pats, which means He can also use you. God does not want you to remain comfortable with being critical of yourself. For far too long, you have comfortably remained outside of His purpose because of this way of thinking. God wants you to walk into ALL that He has for you, but doing so will require a change in perception that is attainable through the power of decreeing. (Read Job 22:28.) What you need to be established in your life must be decreed.

To every "**Pat**," may I invite you to begin a daily "Mirror Moment Decree" that has the power to shift your perception and spirit into the place of purpose. Take time each day to look in the mirror and declare the following:

> God is God; I am not.
> Despite my flaws, He loves me.
> Today, I DECREE
> I trust the Potter for I am but clay.
> Today, I DECREE
> The need to be critical is renounced.
> Today, I DECREE
> God is in control, not me.
> Today, I DECREE
> God speaks, and I listen.
> Today, I DECREE
> "Yes" to God's purpose and "No" to my need to intervene.
> Today, I DECREE
> I am birthing purpose not by might nor by power but by His Spirit (Zechariah 4:6).
> Today, I DECREE
> I trust in the Lord with all of my heart and lean not to my own understanding. In all of my ways I will acknowledge Him and He will direct my path (Proverbs 3:5, 6).

Now pray, trust God and go about your day, knowing that you are on your way to purpose!

B. COVERED

Covereds are more concerned about outward presentation than inward transformation. They conceal their true identity from those around them and struggle to "be themselves." The identities of these individuals are buried under layers of masks, which are used to enhance outer abilities while diminishing inner purpose. This attraction to the superficial deters Covereds from birthing purpose because it is supernatural. Their greatest challenge is identifying what causes them to avoid the internal and attract to the external.

Some common causes include low self-esteem, lack of self-confidence, years of abuse, feelings of insufficiency, inadequacy, insignificance, and so forth. Within every "Covered" is a resistance to face the woman underneath the makeup, the man before the steroids, the person prior to weight-loss surgery, etc. Covereds have trouble facing their own reality and are thereby subject to accept a false reality that they have created for themselves. In order to birth purpose, Covereds must face their reality without any enhancements.

If "Covered" describes you, do not feel offended or dismayed. In spite of your insecurities, God is willing to offer you a deeper awareness of who you are in Him. Doing so will require you to "get real" with yourself so you can "get real" with God. He will then allow you to discover and rediscover your value, worth and security in Christ. What's essential is that your inside matches your outside. What good is it to have a perfect body and a heart filled with bitterness?

To be clear, nothing is wrong with improving one's appearance; however, problems arise when outer appearance devalues the inner person. The good news is that history proves that God accomplishes great works through "COVEREDS" like Moses and Jeremiah who both expressed insecurity when God called them into purpose (Exodus 6:30, Jeremiah 1:6). Surely He can accomplish greater work through you. It is your time to stop hiding behind the cover up and come to the One who covers you!

To every "Covered," may I invite you to begin a daily "Mirror Moment Decree" that has the power to shift your perception and spirit into the place of purpose. Take time each day to look in the mirror and declare the following:

> God made me because He loves me.
> I love me because He loves me.
> Although I make mistakes, I am not a mistake.
> Today, I DECREE
>   I am not a prisoner of anyone's words.
> Today, I DECREE
>   Insecurity and fear is renounced.
> Today, I DECREE
>   Confidence and boldness is received.
> Today, I DECREE
>   Honesty with God, myself and others.
> Today, I DECREE

I will face _____(insert what
you have been avoiding).
Today, I DECREE
 I am fearfully and wonderfully made—
inside and out.
Today, I DECREE
 I am birthing the purpose God has for
my life.
Today, I DECREE
 I will be confident of this very thing that
He that begun a good work in me shall
perform it to the day of Jesus Christ
(Philippians 1:6).

Now pray, trust God and go about your day,
knowing that you are on your way to purpose!

C. MORGAN
 Morgan, Morgan, Morgan—as beautiful,
confident and influential as they want to be; these
are great traits. Morgans are hardworking,
successful and appear to always have everything
under control. Morgans are often overachievers and
unintentionally intimidate those around them.
They struggle to identify growing edges because
they are consumed by past, present and/or future
accomplishments. Morgans can learn valuable
lessons by taking time to hear and receive
constructive criticism. Although nothing is wrong
with being optimistic, birthing purpose requires
the person to confront difficult and even dark
places that success overshadows.
 If you are a Morgan, be assured that
although you are successful, you have not yet

arrived. Take time to consider the areas in your life over which you have total control; these are the areas to which God wants access. God wants to teach you more about your purpose, but because you know so much, you keep missing the lesson. For this reason, Morgan has things on the back burner that should have already been completed.

God wants to birth purpose in every Morgan, but He needs them to get past what they have already accomplished and recognize there is much more to attain in God (1 Corinthians 2:9).

To every Morgan, I invite you to begin a daily "Mirror Moment Decree" that that has the power to shift your perception and spirit into the place of purpose. Take time each day to look in the mirror and declare the following:

> God trusts me with much.
> God chose me for more.
> Today, I DECREE
>   God has total access to every part of my life.
> Today, I DECREE
>   I am humble because everything I have, God gave me.
> Today, I DECREE
>   I will identify my growing edges and outgrow them.
> Today, I DECREE
>   I will learn the lesson God is teaching me.
> Today, I DECREE

I have victory over _____ (Insert what
your success overshadows, e.g., hurt,
guilt, insecurity, etc.).
Today, I DECLARE
I am birthing the purpose God has for
my life.
Today, I DECREE
I will be confident of this very thing that
He that begun a good work in me shall
perform it to the day of Jesus Christ.

Now pray, trust God and go about your day,
knowing that you are on your way to purpose!

D. TIM

Tim is timely. Tims make time for work,
school, friends, family and everyone else except
themselves. Tim is often last on his list. It typically
takes something serious or borderline catastrophic
for Tims to finally take time to care for themselves.
Many Tims lose their sense of self-worth (an
assessment with which a true Tim will, of course,
disagree), but it is accurate for many reasons. For
instance, Tims can count on one hand how many
things they have taken time to do for themselves.
Typically, when Tims plan to do something for
themselves, they end up rescheduling or never
calling to make the appointment to begin with.
Tims' daily to-do list never includes self-care
because they are caretakers. However, caretakers
are no good for anything if they are helpless
themselves. Tims most likely need a vacation—a
real one—not one where they work while cruising!
Self-care also prevents burnout.

Tims who take care of themselves will be healthy vessels through which God can birth purpose.

If you are a Tim, be aware of the fact that purpose requires rest and relaxation. You, my friend, have well-earned both. God even wants that for you! As Psalm 62:1 says *"...my soul finds rest in God..."* When is the last time your emotions, thoughts, or will had a date with divine rest? God is calling you to rest so He can rejuvenate you. The truth is, you would not be as exhausted as you are if you would simply make time to accept God's invitation to rest every now and then. Slow down, take a breath and be still then you will really KNOW He is God (Psalm 46:10). There is much revelation to be gained when you are restful in the presence of the Lord.

To every Tim, I invite you to begin a daily "Mirror Moment Decree" that that has the power to shift your perception and spirit into the place of purpose. Take time each day to look in the mirror and declare the following:

> God has given me this day and time with a purpose in mind.
> Today, I DECREE
> I will operate in God's time, not my own.
> Today, I DECREE
> Busyness, rushing and anxiety are renounced.
> TODAY, I DECREE
> Peace, tranquility and rest are received.
> Today, I DECREE
> I will not fill my day with unproductive tasks.

31

Today, I DECREE
I will not reschedule another
opportunity to be cared for.
Today, I DECREE
I am valuable enough to make time for
me.
Today, I DECREE
I am birthing the purpose God has for
my life.
Today, I DECREE
"Yes" to Matthew 11:28 (HCSB), which
declares, "Come to Me, all of you who are
weary and burdened, and I will give you
rest."

Now pray, trust God and go about your day,
knowing that you are on your way to purpose!

For Letters A-D (ALL)

You have confronted some hard truths, so now take
some more time to pray. Then write in the space
provided what God has revealed to you *about you*
through prayer and the exercise.

_____
_____
_____
_____
_____
_____
_____
_____
_____
_____
_____

_____

_____

_____

_____

Allow me to pose the question one last time: what
do you see when you look in the mirror? This is an
ever-changing answer. May I encourage you to
make time for your daily mirror moments. Notice
how you move between categories from week to
week. Notice your growth, growing edges and
resistance to grow. Do not allow your flaws to
discourage you. Use them as opportunities to
overcome. The bottom line is that your insecurities
will not allow you to see yourself as God sees you.
They can even prevent you from fulfilling God's
purpose for your life. Therefore, cultivate the ability
to name them and the authority to "null and void"
them. Purpose requires consistency. If you develop

a consistent pattern of observing and overcoming

you are on track to birth purpose.

CHAPTER TWO

Emergency

People marvel at the sight of a newborn baby but rarely consider the fact that the new mother enters the jaws of death to give birth. The great trials in our lives produce the greatest triumphs. In the most painful of events God reveals His purpose to us. This is why God oftentimes raises up and uses those once addicted to drugs, alcohol, and sexual sins as His chosen worldwide evangelists.

Purpose requires us to watch the words we use to describe our trials. We are quick to label opposition with words like *deterrent, adversity, challenge* and even *demonic*. As much as we fail to admit it, most of us dislike facing the reality that God's purpose for our lives includes suffering. We sometimes resist our purpose in God because it calls us to experience that which is out of our control. We do not hate suffering because it is too long or because it is unfair; rather, we really loathe suffering because it is out of our control. If we could stop bad situations from happening to good people, we would. If this were possible, we would no longer have approximately 24,000 *non-smokers* in America who annually die of lung cancer.[i]

The truth of the matter is that human beings long to be the CEO, COO and CAO of their daily lives. However, only when we become willing to relinquish total control of our lives can a person honestly say, "I trust God." God is not interested in having limited control; rather, He wants complete access to your emotional, physical, spiritual, personal and financial life. He does not want control because He is domineering; He wants control because He is omnipotent ("all powerful"). God knows that you are not big, strong or wise enough in your own power to control your life. **God has the power to birth purpose in you and sustain you in Him once you get there.** The only way to ensure that you walk into your purpose is to make sure you are walking behind the One who has all power. If you walk in front of Him, you will miss it, mistake it or even force it before its time.

Jesus said in Luke 9:23, "...If any man will come after me, let him deny himself, and take up His cross daily, and follow me." Without getting into a lengthy theological dissertation, I want to draw your attention to two phrases He uses: "*after Me*" and "*follow Me*." You are called to follow Christ; Christ is not called to follow you. You are His disciple—not the other way around. Therefore, there is absolutely no way in the world we can follow Jesus if we are in front of Him. When is the last time you saw a shepherd walking behind his sheep? You must position your will, thoughts, hopes and dreams after Him, which means His plan, His purpose and His will are before your own.

When you are "after" Him, it becomes easier for you to "follow" Him. You will follow His instructions, His Word, His principles and give birth at the right time to the purpose He has put within you.

According to Jeremiah 1:5, God placed purpose within you before conception. Therefore, He alone knows precisely what your purpose entails. He knows exactly how to get you to your purpose. Why would you not follow the One who has the directions to get you to your destination? If only following Him were as natural to us as breathing, then God would not have to allow adversity to occur in order to get us in the right position. Nevertheless, when God needs something to emerge from your spirit, He will do whatever it takes to get your attention.

One cold Wednesday morning in December of 2015, I went to the doctor's office after experiencing very blurry vision in my right eye for about two weeks. Like every other non-physician who self-diagnoses, I attributed the problem to stress related to my busy schedule and supposed it would go away. To my surprise, this was not to be the case.

Following the urging of my mother and my increasing fear while driving, I decided to make an appointment with the eye doctor. Little did I know that this appointment would change my life as I knew it. I assumed that he would say all I needed to do was use some drops, and everything would be better in the morning. However, when I sat in the chair as the doctor seemingly stretched my eye in ways I had no idea it could stretch, I was bombarded by many different emotions. The loudest one was fear. Fear screamed through each heartbeat as it became harder to breathe due to the pressure the doctor put on my eye. To make measures worse, the piercing bright light he used felt like I had taken an accidental glance into the Caribbean sun without any sunglasses on the hottest day of summer. The pressure intensified as he pressed down into my eyeball, forcing my pupil to go in various directions. I felt like crying because the procedure was so invasive.

I felt like leaving because I was intimidated by the terms he named to his assistant that sounded like a foreign language. He was speaking English but using words that happened to be completely unfamiliar to me. I tried my best to relax by tapping my fingers on the side of the examining chair. I desperately tried to avoid allowing my anxiety to overwhelm me to the point that he could not finish the examination.

After all of the "foreign language" ceased, the doctor spoke to me in plain English. "The retina in your right eye has detached and requires emergency surgery—on Friday."

This report meant I only had two days to process, prepare and go into surgery! Needless to say, my heart felt like it was ready to explode, and my lungs felt as though they were closing. As I think back to that appointment, I believe I was experiencing what could have been an anxiety attack; however, by the grace of God, it did not happen. After the examination, the assistant took my mom and I back to the waiting room. As soon as

I sat down, I lost it. A sea of tears streamed down my face. I felt emotionally assaulted by the overwhelming fear that paralyzed me and the worry that arrested me. I had no idea what to expect. I had never before had surgery, and now in only two days, I had to schedule eye surgery. All I could think about were the responses to the questions I had asked in the room about the procedure to reattach my retina.

From what I understood, I would not be fully under the effects of anesthesia. A massive needle would be inserted into my eye to release a gas bubble. As these thoughts raced through my mind, I became that five-year-old little girl who was in desperate need of her mother's touch. My mother held my hand and wiped my tears as I broke down in the waiting room. All I could think about were the "what if's" of the surgery. *What if there's an accident? What if he's wrong—even though he gave the second opinion? What if they're both wrong? Where did this come from?* Although I had already asked and learned detached retinas were fairly common for nearsighted persons, the answer simply was not a good enough answer for me.

The doctor had provided a very clinical answer explaining that detached retinas occur when the vitreous fluid in the eye leaks through a retinal hole or tear and collects underneath the retina. The overabundance of fluid buildup literally peels the retina away from the tissue, detaching it. The area where the retina is detached loses it blood supply and stops working, causing the loss of vision.

Even though I had the facts, they only added to my fear. After leaving the office, I cried more and more. My mother lovingly held my hand and assured me that God would carry me through. I cannot imagine what my life would have been like if I had had to experience that diagnosis on my own. After careful consideration, I realized it would not be feasible to have the surgery in only two days because I needed to finish my last semester of seminary, and I was so close to finishing. I was in the seventh week of an eight-week semester that would conclude my graduate studies. I refused to receive an "incomplete" from my uncompromising professor who was aware of my emergency but showed no compassion.

Nevertheless, I took that Thursday, Friday, Saturday and Sunday to do two weeks' worth of work. Yes, you read that right. In only four days, with one blurry eye, a gallon and a half of determination and an infinite amount of grace, I completed all of the papers and exams necessary for graduation. I was able to graduate in May of 2016 purely by grace. Honestly speaking, the substantial workload was next to humanly impossible to complete. However, I embraced a coping mechanism, which is known in the beautiful world of chaplaincy as *avoidance*. This method of coping occurs when one consciously or unconsciously focuses on a task in order to avoid processing fears, anxieties and worries. Therefore, in order to escape confronting those difficult emotions tied to the anticipated eye surgery, I began to address all of the other external areas in my life including schoolwork, buying Christmas gifts and anything else that brought me away from reality for a moment.

I simply could not process how I would undergo emergency eye surgery only days after accepting a new position that offered double the salary I was currently earning. Financially, I worried how my bills would be paid and whether or not the job would be available after I recovered. Additionally, I had lost my part-time job due to downsizing, so I really needed this job. I planned to move out of state, start the new job and begin a new chapter of my life. Everything seemed crystal clear until now. Needless to say, I had to reassess my entire life as I knew it, especially since the doctor had said my recovery could take anywhere between one to six months, depending on how my eye reacted to the surgery. Despite my many days of worrying, one night changed everything.

The night before the surgery, I wrapped myself in my prayer shawl, laid prostrate before the Lord drowned in emotions, and something unforgettable happened. As I laid there, I had no idea what to say. All I could think of was the fact that a needle would be inserted into my eye within the next six to seven hours. Without saying a word, I simply cried out to God. The more I cried, the more I felt the presence of the Lord upon me. In the midst of my tears, I anointed my eye and asked the Lord to heal me so that I would not have to go through the surgery.

As I was praying, the Lord spoke to me and said, "You always pray the same prayer. You always pray, "Lord, let me see as you see." This is how you will see as I see."

He continued, "I look down on the world, and I see pain and that pains Me. I see hurt, and that hurts Me. As in the natural, so in the spirit. I will allow the surgery to take place on your right eye. You must experience pain in the natural and pain in the spirit so you will be able to see as I see. Therefore, you must trust that I will carry you through this time. This situation is of much spiritual significance in your life and your ministry. You are praying for Me to take you out of this, when you really should be praying for Me to take you into it. You should be praying for Me to take you deeper because in suffering, you will see Me. In pain, you will hear Me. In the discomfort of fear and anxiety, you will learn to trust Me above all. In this place of pain, you have come to know Me, and you will come to know Me even more. I have chosen you to go through this before the foundation of the world was formed. Trust Me."

In that moment I realized what I had been looking at as adversity was really a privilege waiting to be perceived. God had found me worthy to suffer something for the sake of the Gospel. I felt such a weight lifted off of my spirit man, and the true peace of God overtook me that night. I literally felt my heart slow down and beat at a relaxed rate. I took a deep breath and felt the presence of the Lord throughout my entire being.

Peace, not panic, is a key ingredient for purpose. You must seek His peace no matter how overwhelming the rigors of life becomes. His peace led me to record my voice speaking this chapter onto my cell phone the very same night of my eye surgery. With one eye closed shut under a plastic cover sealed with tape to ensure immobility and light resistance, I knew I had to finish this chapter. As I listened to the playback, my words seemed ambiguous because of the pain medication I was given. However, against ALL odds, I knew purpose was calling, and I had to answer.

I would have never been able to write this book if it was not for this emergency. As I have mentioned, God gave me this book in 2012, and I kept putting everything else before it, but this time it was different. God showed me that He will allow an emergency situation to occur when there is an urgency in the Spirit. Something about an emergency causes what is inside of a person to come out. I liken it to times when people run into burning buildings to rescue a child on the fifteenth floor without any thought of the dangers in their way or of their own safety. The purpose of saving that innocent child overrules all adversity. Likewise, God uses emergency situations to ensure your purpose will overall all odds.

I had to endure great pressure in order to get this book out of my spirit. Likewise, you will face pressure on the road to birthing purpose. Do not allow the pressure to scare you, but use it to your advantage. Change your perspective on how you view the pressure, the pain or the opposition and see the situation in the way God sees it—the vehicle in which you need to travel to reach your place of purpose. God knows how much you can take, and even when you think it is unbearable, trust Him.

Finishing my master's degree was not something I did because I needed it for my career. Rather, I began working on the degree before I knew I needed it because it was in my spirit to complete. This urgency to complete my degree is why I postponed the surgery until my studies were finished. Years later, having a master's degree happened to be a requirement for the job I desired. I did not know it, but purpose did. Purpose will cause you to fulfill requirements before you even know they are required. Completing my master's was a divinely appointed part of God's molding of my ministry through education. If you are going to go after purpose, you may lose your sight, mobility, friends, family or anything else you hold dear;

however, your losses will never outweigh your gains. Rest assured, God honors sacrifice and suffering, so no matter what you lose, He will restore.

Mandate to Isolate

After the surgery, while lying in my bed that night with my eyes shut, it felt as if a siren went off in my spirit. Silence surrounded me, and stillness overtook me. I had no choice but to listen, but not to people or music or even my own thoughts but to the voice of God. I had no access to my phone, computer or the outdoors because my eye could not tolerate any light. I was separated from family and friends because I needed to rest in order for my eye to heal properly.

God then spoke to me and said, "This is a mandate to isolate."

I finally got the picture. *This is the place God has been trying to get me to for years! But I kept filling what should have been God's time with the busyness of my life.* In my hospital bed, God opened my mind to a new understanding of isolation. I thought for sure I already understood isolation when God called me into ministry and I lost a few friends, disappointed some family members and received criticism from acquaintances, but I realized those times did not represent isolation. I was merely experiencing separation, level 1 or the gentle beginning.

Isolation was a whole new level that required something that I was not used to, was not prepared for and did not see coming. When God needed to get Jonah to purpose, he caused a whale to swallow him (Jonah 1:17). For three days and three nights, Jonah was in a place he was not used to, was not prepared for and did not see coming.

The way God got Jonah's attention is one of two ways He may use to bring you into purpose. Sometimes the Lord ushers in the person easily like Simon Peter and Andrew to whom He simply said, *"...Follow me, and I will make you fishers of men"* (Matthew 4:19), and they immediately obeyed. At other times, He ushers in a person using drastic measures as in the case of Jonah. Either way He puts you in a place where He has your full attention. Jonah was mandated to isolation in the belly of a whale. His attempt to flee the presence of the Lord may suggest he was trying to run away from his purpose.

True purpose is only found in the presence of the Lord. Being detached from the presence of the Lord meant he would be detached from his purpose. Jonah's purpose including going to Nineveh; however, if he had never entered the belly of the whale, he would have never made it there. In essence, the belly of the whale was the prerequisite to his purpose.

Have you identified the prerequisite to your purpose? Perhaps it was the sickness, the loss of a loved one or the failed marriage that was meant to capture your attention. Once you identify it, do not get trapped there; that was merely level 1. God wants to move you to your next level of purpose, but He needs your willingness to shut out everything, everybody and shut yourself in with Him.

As opinionated, independent and as free as human beings are, when it comes to a mandate from God, all of that goes out the window. A *mandate* really means an order or a command.[1] Simply put, you really do not have a choice in the matter. God sets aside specific periods in our lives that require isolation so He can instruct, influence and provide you with insight from Him alone. When God calls you to a time of isolation, it will cost you some things, including relationships, jobs, friends and even social activities. However, the revelation you will receive from the Creator while in isolation will be incomparable to any amount of time you could have spent with creation. Isolation opens your mind to the reality that God has called you to something great which outweighs the backlash you will receive from people who think you should be available when they call. Isolation produces an anointing called "No." You enter into a place where "no" truly means no.

Along with the anointing to say "No" comes the ability to set intentional boundaries with friends and family. Setting perimeters requires ignoring phone calls, not responding to text messages, not attending events or simply not giving up the time that was set aside to be in the presence of the Lord. This may sound extreme to some, but God wants one-on-one time with his child. Those who have been sensing this desire in their spirit will understand that the benefits always far outweigh the burdens. Intentional boundaries are necessary for purpose.

When is the last time you intentionally set aside time to listen for God's voice? When is the last time you gave God your undivided attention? Church does not count because more likely than not, you were on your phone at some point during the service. Let's get real, even in God's house we do not give God our undivided attention. We focus on insignificant, shallow and fleshly things like who is wearing the best suit, who sang the best solo or who gave the biggest offering.

Woe unto us! When we are in the house of God, the least WE can do is give God our full attention. Perhaps we can start by turning off our cell phones in the service and focusing on the reason why we gathered in the first place—Christ. Be assured your flesh will reject that last line, but remember what we established in the beginning of this book: when resistance in your flesh rises up, it should serve as your confirmation that God is speaking to your spirit man. The question is: will you receive His instruction? Do you know how much power we would experience in the body of Christ worldwide if we were all on one accord and determined to be intentional about not being distracted from the presence of the Lord? We would see a weekly outpouring of God's Spirit. Perhaps if we banned cell-phone usage for the mere one-to-four hours we spend in church, we too could have an upper-room experience. The same God who shook the upper room will also shake our churches if we intentionally focus on Him.

The eyes of the Divine sees what others may consider a "loss" as a gain. When God anoints you to say "No" and you set intentional boundaries, God will lead you to a place where His mandate will mean more to you than life itself. Perhaps this is the place where Paul was when he said, *"For to me to live is Christ, and to die is gain"* (Philippians 1:21, ESV). He was so in touch with the mandate that he came to a place where he marveled at the fact that his very existence was possible because of Christ, and that, my friend, is where isolation will also drive you. You will stop taking for granted what you should marvel in awe of. I believe it is safe to say that Paul had a "mandate mentality." No matter what the mandate cost him, he was willing to live or die to fulfill its demands because in both, God received the glory.

Unfamiliar and Uncomfortable

Three to four days after my eye surgery, I began to notice a black spot to the bottom right of my eye. I thought something had gone wrong in the surgery, so I went to see my doctor. He explained that the circle I saw was the gas bubble that had been inserted into my eye prior to attaching the retina. He had neglected to tell me that the gas bubble would rupture into minute particles that would literally bounce around in the fluid of my eye.

This process took place over the following days, which caused me to feel goosebumps or "skeeved out" as I like to call it whenever I opened my eyes during the day. I liken what was happening to watching something on television that makes you want to itch. I thought I would be able to relax in bed after my surgery and focus on healing and hearing from God, but this unfamiliar and uncomfortable sight made resting extremely difficult. *What more can I bear? A detached retina, emergency eye surgery, finishing my last paper with one eye taped shut, post-surgery pains? Shouldn't I be on the "okay, that's-enough" list in God's mind?* Apparently not.

After about 72 hours of suffering, the phenomena became so bad that I had to use a little ingenuity. I taped a piece of dark construction paper over my post-surgery glasses during the day. Everything became black so I would not be able to see the little black circles dancing around my eye. Relief, at last!

Here's the lesson God taught me from those dancing spots: I was comfortable talking to Him because that was familiar. I was uncomfortable listening for God when I encountered the unfamiliar. Once again, not one time did I pray and listen for God's for instruction when I faced what made me uncomfortable.

How often do you seek God when something makes you uncomfortable? Oftentimes, we react in our flesh without even considering what God has to say about the situation. Purpose calls you to the experience the unfamiliar and even the uncomfortable in order to teach you how to respond. Your response could determine whether or not you bring forth your purpose.

This is why it is important not to put the cart before the horse. Do not think that you have already arrived at the end of the battle while bullets are still flying past your face. I truly believed that my test was over, and I had received the revelation and that this time of isolation would be alone without God. However, I did not consider the fact that I had more lessons to be learned and victories to be won. God is never finished teaching any of His children. So stick around long enough to learn the lesson until the uncomfortable and unfamiliar becomes comfortable and familiar.

Eye Training 101

Nearly three weeks post-surgery, the bubble had finally disappeared; however, I could only open my eye about 50 percent. Of course, this inability limited my visual range, and I could see nothing over my head or in my peripheral view. Not being able to see above me meant I had to constantly remember to lift my head higher, which I found awkward because I could see clearly with my left eye. When raising my head to adjust, I felt off-balance. The worst part was when I would look down or bend down, my entire eye would go black.

A number of times I nearly hit the floor, trying to pick up something that I had dropped. I became fearful of bending down because of the dizzy sensation and uncertainty of whether or not I would find myself on the floor with what I was trying to pick up.

After numerous doctor's appointments and being informed that mine was a "slow healing process," I knew I had to do something if I wanted to be able to carry out normal daily activities. So, I began to do my own form of physical therapy. I would do 15 to 20 reps of moving my eye left to right, up and down, clockwise and counterclockwise. I did not feel like I was making much progress because when I looked at my eye after the exercise, it would still only appear to be about 50 percent open. However, I kept doing the reps. After nearly three more weeks, I regained the ability to see above my head without looking up. *Progress, at last!*

As of this writing, one year has passed, and I still continue this practice. Although my vision has not returned to what it was before the surgery and my right eye is still blurry, thanks to the self-taught physical therapy, I have regained my peripheral vision. My eye is now 100 percent open. This practice of eye training truly made a world of difference because I met someone who had the same exact surgery around the time I underwent mine, and his eye is still only 50 percent open. When we were discussing the problem, I asked, "Have you tried to move it around?"

He replied, "It never even occurred to me to try such a thing."

Without the working of the muscles, I believe my eye too would have remained 50 percent closed or droopy. However, I possessed the will to see my world. Purpose demands this same will to see it come to pass, especially when it looks like it is impossible to see. You must train your eye to see what God has for you. With limited vision, you can easily misinterpret God's purpose for your life; however, if you take the time to work at developing your visual muscles, you will see purpose more clearly. With clear vision, there is nothing you cannot accomplish. *"Where there is no vision, the people perish..."* (Proverbs 29:18), which means their purpose perishes with them. On the other hand, where there is vision, the people thrive, which means their purpose thrives.

Have you trained your eye to see the vision? If you cannot see the vision, purpose dies. If it is dead already, retrain your eye to see the vision so that it will live again! Purpose requires eye training.

In Jeremiah 1:11, God showed the prophet a vision then asked him *"what seest thou?"* and he responded, *"I see a rod of an almond tree."* The meaning of the word *seest* in this verse is "perceive or inspect."[ii] To *perceive* is to notice something that typically escapes the attention of other people.[iii] To *inspect* is to examine something carefully. God was literally asking Jeremiah to name with precision and without error exactly what He was revealing to His prophet. There was no time to do a long examination; he was required to immediately discern what he was seeing with accuracy. Jeremiah did not struggle or misinterpret the request because his eye was trained, which is exactly why the Lord replies, *"...Thou hast well seen: for I will hasten my word to perform it."*

Purpose requires the child of God to see well. How many dreams and/or visions has God shown you that you have seen in error? No wonder it has not come to pass. After God had affirmed Jeremiah's eye had perceived accurately, **then** He said, *"...I will hasten my word to perform it."* God wants to accelerate His word concerning your life, but you have failed to train your eye to see properly. God is looking to speed up the manifestation of your vision, but every time He shows you something, instead of seeing it, you come up with ways to see yourself out of it.

For instance, God shows you a vision of your owning your own business. Instead of preparing for the business, you begin to talk yourself out of it with excuses like "I do not have a degree in business administration," or "It costs too much" or "I do not have any experience." You need eye training! If God shows you something, He wants to hasten His word to perform it. God wants to give it to you so badly that He has tried, retried, prophesied and re-prophesied the same thing, but you still refuse to see it.

The time has come for you to see well, Jeremiah. Stop looking at what you do not have, who you do not know, what your family background is or what your bank account says! Trust the God who gave you the vision will hasten and perform it! God is waiting to release the provision you need, but it will take you training your eye to see well in order to receive it.

Matthew 6:22 (NASB) says, *"The eye is the lamp of the body; so then if your eye is clear, your whole body will be full of light."* Your eye directly impacts the rest of your body, determining not only what you see but what you know. Naturally, when you see a dog, you know you are seeing a dog. Spiritually, you know God is God, but you cannot see Him. Or can you? He did reveal Himself to Isaiah the prophet in Isaiah chapter 6. Yet the apostle John writes that no man has ever seen God except the Son of God (John 1:18) The Bible is not contradictory because Isaiah saw Him in a vision, which is a spiritual, as opposed to physical, reality. Isaiah immediately recognized his own unworthiness when he saw with his spiritual eye. This means what your spiritual eye perceives determines how your flesh responds.

When you look with a spiritual eye, you can see an overdrawn bank account as a check for $1,000,000 waiting to clear. How are you looking at your current realities? What you perceive with your spiritual eye will never make sense, but it will always make faith.

You must be willing to keep working the same muscles until they are strong enough to do what they were created to do. My eyes and yours were created to see. If you take the time to ensure you are actively working to perfect the vision God has given to you, I can promise that you will bring it forth.

How do you train your eye? Read the Word of God daily; better yet, study the Word of God daily. Studying allows you to develop a keen awareness to the voice of God. Once you know His voice, you will clearly and accurately be able to see the vision He puts before you. You will not fall subject to making good decisions; rather, you will opt to making God decisions. The more you study, the more you will perceive what *looks like* God from what actually *IS* God.

When your vision is challenged, do not retreat. Train harder, research more, study deeper and watch what God does! Do your part, and God will do His! Without the ability to see anything above me, I was constantly faced with the reminder that my eye was still in recovery. Simply because something is in recovery does not mean it will not recover! Do not be discouraged when you find your vision is not fully recovered, but is in recovery because that means it is, in fact, *recovering*. What have you walked away from because it was recovering? Think on it and get back to work!

Take a REST

American society teaches us the more we do, the more successful we will become. The harder you work, the more you will achieve. I challenge that theory with what may seem like an oxymoron: if you want to produce something great, you need to sleep more. We put endless amounts of energy into making sure our businesses are successful, our companies are prosperous and our income increases only to become discouraged when life does not go our way. Have you ever wondered how you could put your all into something and still feel as though it could have gone better? This reaction is the result of never considering that we need to take a rest. Let me state this probability as nicely as possible: you may be overdoing it.

To all of the overachievers who "go hard" for this and that, this thought may be alarming to you. But consider this: when you spend more time in preparation than you do in prayer for an event you are leading, then you have overdone it. It is easy to rely on your own strength because you know what you are capable of achieving. However, it is harder to rely on God because you do not know what God will do. **Your expectation should never exceed your impartation,** which means, you should never expect more from God when you have spent less time in His presence. You need time to rest in the presence of the Lord in order to adequately talk to and hear from Him.

Only God can do exceedingly and abundantly above all we can ask or think according to the power that works within us; therefore, in order to achieve something greater than our own expectations, we must be willing to rest in God and receive instruction, insight and innovation. I would not have finished this book had I not taken time to rest in the presence of the Lord. If you take time to rest in the presence of the Lord, your vision will not meet your expectation instead God will exceed it

Without the ability to see, the only thing I could do was speak to God and hear from Him. God chose you and I to be in His presence, it is no wonder why things go array when we do not seek Him. This is why whenever God wants you to produce something in the Earthly realm, you must rest in the Lord. Had I continued in the busyness of my life's schedule, I would not have received clear instruction from God on what to include in this book. Therefore, purpose requires rest. God did not show Joseph his purpose while he was feeding his flock; rather, it was while he was resting. God revealed His purpose to Joseph in a dream. If you want to dream, you need to sleep. If you want to manifest that dream, you need to sleep harder. **Resting in God will give you supernatural access to what is naturally unavailable.**

It was not until my entire being was confined to a bed without the care of any to-do list that my heart caught up with God's. It was in resting, sometimes in total silence that I could hear the heartbeat of God for souls, the downtrodden, the seriously ill, the elderly, etc. God called me to many nights and mornings of intercessory prayer for strangers that He would show me when my eyes were closed. God knew that if I continued in the busyness of my normal schedule, I would have never made as much time for intercessory prayer. I had developed not just a habit but a lifestyle of praying five to seven times a day.

I am sharing this in the hopes of awakening a hunger in you to rest in the presence of the Lord. During this time of rest, I felt closer than ever to the Lord and truly in line with His purpose for my life. In solitude I heard clear instructions from the Lord. God will download unheard-of inventions, untried plans and uncommon ideas that will benefit His kingdom in a way for which man could never take the glory. God wants to release unique strategies to you, but He is waiting for you to rest in His presence.

Stop resting in idleness, busyness, and foolishness. Allow the Lord to show you what to do before you take another step or make another decision. Stop operating from a place of anxiousness and learn to operate from a place of rest. *Rest* does not merely mean to physically sleep, it also means to be still. How many minutes in your day are you still? Most of us cannot even think of one minute when we are still enough to hear the voice of God. Let this serve as your reminder to make time to rest in the presence of the Lord. Don't you want to know what God wants to say to you before another prophet has to come and tell you? Well, following this principle is how you find out. Feel free to put down this book and go rest in the presence of the Lord. Tune everything out and listen for His voice.

What did God say to you?

_____

_____

_____

_____

_____

_____

_____

_____

CHAPTER THREE

Enemy

The womb is the place where a baby is conceived, nurtured and kept safe until the time comes to give birth. Anything that threatens the baby's birth is an enemy.

Consider how often have you actually been able to go into a grocery store and leave with only the one item you went in for? Most people are unable to leave with purchasing only that one lemon needed to tenderize the chicken waiting at home without picking up extra items along the way. Many fall subject to sales, advertisements, coupons and whatever else happens to capture their attention. The same is often true regarding the purpose of God for your life.

God has placed a divine purpose way down on the inside of your spirit that you have yet to unlock because you have been distracted. That's right, you have been distracted by all of the shiny fruit on sale around you in the supermarket of your soul. All of the variety of desserts, cereals and potato chips have consistently caused you to miss that one lemon you went into the store to purchase. How many more times will you return home without the lemon? With this illustration, God is saying, "My child, as long as you keep stopping to look at everything else, you will never tap into that one lemon in your soul that needs to be squeezed to life."

This purpose of God within the depths of your soul always gets overlooked because everything else is easier to reach. Indeed, you have to walk to get the lemon, but you think about, grab and purchase chocolate bars because you only had to stand where they were. In other words, when you are in a stagnant place, you have easier access to everything you do not need. However, momentum opens the door to purpose. Are you willing to move?

If you want to birth purpose, you must stop standing in the same place. You must also fight against the urge to handle matters haphazardly! Fight your way through the supermarket of your own soul. Fight to resist every wet floor sign that causes you to take the longer way to your destination. Fight every "spill on aisle 9" that forces you to take a different aisle that you did not intend to navigate. Fight to not spend your hard-earned money on useless sweets that will only cause cavities in your soul. In order to birth God's purpose, you must resist any distraction in your life.

Distractions will make you unfruitful in the very season God intends for you to bear fruit. Distractions cause you to lose focus when God is vying for your attention. When you start to do the research for the project God wants you to start, a family member dies, causing you to walk away from your study. Two years pass, and you never pick it up again, which is precisely what happened to me.

When I started to write this book in 2012, my father died unexpectedly, my mother faced a near-death experience, and my grandmother died suddenly—all in a time span of only six months. These events shook my world, numbed my soul and caused me to fall into a depression that lasted for nearly a year. I abandoned the Master of Divinity program in which I was enrolled at Liberty University because I lost the desire to do anything constructive. I did not even want to speak to people. I felt dead on the inside.

The complicated grieving process, though necessary, distracted me from writing this book. I lost all of my ambition to complete what I had started, and once again, a part of my purpose was placed on the backburner. I fell subject to the spirit of distraction in the supermarket of my own soul. My emotions, thoughts and desires were all distorted because of the intensity of the grief I experienced.

In the midst of my heartaches and tears, God reminded me of a scripture He had given me a few months prior to my personal devastation found in Exodus 20:21, which refers to God's being present in thick darkness. The truth that God was present with me—even in thick darkness ignited the light in my soul to shine again. I knew that since God was with me, I was going to come out of that low place because His light would dispel all of the darkness that had overtaken me.

The overwhelming reality of these traumatic events had distorted my own sense of normalcy; yet the awareness of the light caused me to fight to create a new normal. Yes, my life would never be the same again however I chose to live again. I refused to die on the inside any longer. I chose not only to live but to thrive and go after everything God had for me. I knew these events had happened for a divine reason and believed wholeheartedly that God had left me here for a divine purpose. So, I decided to go after it with everything I had.

About one year later, I reapplied for the Master of Divinity program only to be denied three times, but I refused to quit. I kept challenging the school board's denials for re-admittance into the program until I was finally fully re-enrolled. At last, I was able to pick up where I had left off. Beginning again was not easy, but against all odds, I graduated with honors in the same program I was thrice denied. I can confidently declare to you, in spite of everything you face on your journey to purpose— YOU WILL MAKE IT!

Remember, the soul is the place where our

emotions, thoughts and decisions are made. For this reason, purpose requires your emotions, thoughts and decisions to be filtered through God's Word so you will not fall subject to distractions. What is distracting you? What has arrested your attention? Take time right now to ask God to show it to you if the Spirit has not already brought the matter to your attention. What has kept that book lying dormant in your spirit? What has stopped the women's support group from starting? What has caused the men's mentoring group to fall apart?

I want to invite you to close this book right now, get a pen and paper or perhaps your journal and begin to write in detail the "lemon" or the part of your purpose that you have left in the supermarket. Go on the Internet and begin to research, brainstorm, find out what you need and then pick up this book again later.

THE SPIRIT OF DISTRACTION

Wealthy, powerful King Solomon was the wisest man in the Bible after Christ, yet he possessed a major character flaw, which led to his demise. Though some might think otherwise, that flaw was not the women or concubines, money, popularity or prestige. What led to Solomon's demise was his falling subject to the spirit of distraction. In the beginning, Solomon reaped many blessing as he ascended the throne after his father David. Toward the end of his reign, Solomon did not follow the commandments of God, and at the end of his life, the king articulated much regret for his wasted years as the book of Ecclesiastes reveals.

He expressed great despair after realizing he had spent many years living a life of purposelessness, which is exactly what the spirit of distraction will result in—a life of purposelessness.

Can you imagine how much more joyful the book of Ecclesiastes would have been if Solomon had actually stayed true to the plan, purpose and promises of the Lord? I would imagine his life would have been much like our own lives—less chaotic, overwhelming and stressful. The absence of peace is a telltale sign of someone who has fallen subject to distraction. If you find yourself without peace, you must assess where your mind is and what has been consuming it. The spirit of distraction has entered in one way or another.

This spirit causes people to go to the grave without leaving a legacy because they never finished the project that God had purposed for them to complete. This spirit causes people to repeat the same bad habit year after year and decade after decade. Quite often when people are on their death beds, they compile a mental list of regrets. Most, if not all, have ties to the spirit of distraction. Trust me, my friend, this does not have to be your story!

So how can the spirit of distraction be counteracted? First, you have to acknowledge it is present in your life. Whenever Jesus encountered a demon, He did not ignore it; rather, He acknowledged it. The greatest weapon the Enemy has is making us think he is *not* there. But if you can identify this spirit, you have won half the battle. Satan's second greatest weapon is to make us think he is *always* there. The fact remains that Satan, demons, powers and principalities are all very real; however, they are not omnipresent. Only God has the ability to be everywhere at the same time. Satan does not have that ability. You must know your enemy's weaknesses, his lack of omnipresence is one of his. He is limited and cannot be everywhere at the same time. Therefore, every bad thing that happens in your life cannot be attributed to the Devil. Even if it is a satanic attack, He must go to God to receive permission to attack you as the story of Job teaches us. Therefore, he really is not as powerful as we sometimes make him out to be.

I have to sometimes wonder how many times a day the Devil is confused when he hears his name being spoken. He frequently receives the blame in instances like, "The Devil made my house burn down" when, in reality, you forgot to turn off the pot on the stove. Stop giving him more power than he has. You have authority over him; you simply need to know how to use it.

The following are some ways God gave me to exercise authority over the spirit of distraction or any other spirit working against you:

1.   *Seek God by developing a targeted prayer life*. Stop praying vague prayers! I can prove that God works in specifics. Look at the instructions He gave Noah for the ark or Moses for the tabernacle. God did not include one vague detail; every instruction was clear and precise. Distinct and definite is how your prayer life must be. Distractions often make our prayers unclear and even powerless. If you are looking to manifest your purpose in the earth, you will encounter warfare,

and spiritual warfare calls for you to be focused. It calls you out of the mundane, thoughtless, repetitive prayer that you have prayed all of your life. Warfare should shift your prayer life in a way that brings about a sense of urgency.

You need to be specific in your prayer time. Do not be vague. Perhaps this is why some of your prayers are unanswered today; you lack precision in your prayer life. Ask God to lead you toward what needs to be targeted in prayer. It could be the spirit of distraction, the spirit of laziness, the spirit of anxiety or perhaps another. Discerning this matter is between you and the Lord. A targeted prayer life is built on not "missing God" in prayer and ensures your never praying amiss again. Develop consistency. Set aside specific times you want to pray and follow that schedule. Your spirit man will be built up so when you are faced with adversity, you will know what to pray.

When you are intentionally specific in your prayer life like Hannah was, nothing can be withheld from you. God promised that "...*no good thing will he withhold from them that walk uprightly* (Psalm 84:11). Therefore, a person who possesses an intentional prayer life has taken time to seek God because of his desire to be in the will of God. This desire coupled with a targeted prayer life brings forth results. In 1 Samuel 1:1-20, the Bible says that Hannah received exactly what she asked for because she was sincere and had a specific target in her prayer. If praying specifically worked for Hannah, it will also work for you!

2.	*Identify where the spirit of distraction is present in your life.* The Bible clearly states that

God's people perish for lack of knowledge. This verse covers many aspects of life, including spiritual knowledge. Not knowing where this spirit is present in your life means it will remain there and cause your purpose to perish. The Enemy works best when he is in the dark; expose the light of awareness on him and watch him flee! You can identify where this spirit resides by focusing on where you encounter it while attempting to do what God says. It could be anywhere from in your mind to in your surroundings. Make a mental note, write it down or create a list so the next time you see it, you have the opportunity to dismiss it. This is crucial because it helps you to break the pattern of distraction and establish the pattern of purpose.

3.   *Find an accountability partner.* Then,

yours will not be a solo effort to consciously pursue

God's purpose for your life but a joint effort. Find a

responsible Christian with a strong prayer life.

Look for someone who you feel is more grounded

than you are. Get real with yourself. Sidebar: if you

are the most spiritually mature person in your inner

circle, you need a new circle. You need someone

who is not on the same spiritual plane as you are.

Simply put, an addict cannot help another addict

stop using, but an addiction counselor can. You will

be able to provide one another with tangible

wisdom from experience and sound truths from

God's Word that will promote deliverance. There is

power in agreement. As God's spiritual army, we

must never feel that we have to fight alone or think

that it is wise to fight alone. The Bible affirms this

principle in Matthew 18:19, which says, *"Again I say to you, That if any two of you shall agree on earth as touching anything that they shall ask, it shall be done for them of my Father which is in heaven."* Now for those of you who need to be in control and need to be the most powerful person in the room, this plan will not work for you because you will fight against accountability. Having an accountability partner will only work for those who can recognize they are flawed, can own up to their mistakes, can learn from another and can own the fact that they need more self-control in certain areas of their life.

4. ***Submit and resist.*** When you are unwavering in your submission to God, the spirit of distraction will leave you. James 4:7 says, *"Submit yourselves therefore to God. Resist the devil, and he will flee* *from you.*" The word *submit* in this verse means "to be under obedience," [iv] which indicates you possess a willingness to do what God says. By placing yourself under obedience to God's instruction (i.e., open the business, start the practice, etc.), you stand in agreement with His purpose for your life. Your agreeing with God sends a signal to the spirit of distraction that its time and ownership in your life has expired. Spirits are subject to God, and they know it. My question for you is: do you know it? If so, then use God's Word to counteract the spirit of distraction or any spirit that you encounter while manifesting God's purpose for your life. The more you submit to God, the more you exercise authority over the powers of darkness, rendering them powerless on your road to purpose. It becomes easier to resist the Devil when you are submitted to

God. A person who walks in submission to God cannot easily be overtaken in battle, which is why the Enemy tries to distract you from submitting to God because he knows the more you are submitted, the more he is resisted.

Once you submit, you can resist. *Resist* literally means "to set one's self against, to withstand; to oppose."[v] When you resist, you stand in disagreement with the Enemy, which moves you closer to your purpose. When Jesus was tempted by Satan in Matthew chapter 4, He stood in firm disagreement with the Enemy, thus illustrating the power of resistance. If He would have agreed with even one of Satan's offers, He would have aborted His purpose. However, Christ opposed him by the Word of God, which is the only power great enough to command Satan to flee. By using the

Word to resist the Enemy, Christ moved closer to His purpose of reconciling fallen creation back to their forgiving Creator. If you want to be free from the spirit of distraction, you must agree to submit to God and resist the Devil—the only way this Enemy will flee from you. Are you ready to submit?

5.   *Know your enemy.* When I was in high school, I ran track and field under the direction of one of the greatest coaches on Long Island. He knew track statistics and records like the back of his hand. He was extremely informed of our competitors and even the potential points per event they would achieve long before the meet began. By being so knowledgeable, he was able to see exactly where our team needed to score the most points per event in order to maximize our chances of winning

the meet. He knew the stats of our opponents because he took time to research and record them. He produced more nationally, state and county ranked champions than any other coach on Long Island because he did his homework, mastered his craft and produced greatness. Gaining knowledge is a key to birthing purpose. You *must* know your enemy, but not only know them, you must additionally study them; understand them; and know their strengths, weaknesses and even their potential. When you learn how they can impact you, you find ways to deter them.

Gaining knowledge of your enemy helps you to uncover the tools you need to win not only the battle but the war. I liken the gathering of knowledge to learning a foreign language. You cannot expect to speak Spanish fluently if you never take time to learn it, study it and practice until you perfect it. Similarly, while you learn your enemy (through study, research and experience), you will not only speak purpose fluently, but you will birth it fully. You will become so accustomed to bringing forth what God has put on the inside of you until it becomes a perfected practice, a lifestyle.

6. *Know Your Weapons.* After a period of fasting and prayer, the Lord revealed these eight enemies of purpose to me: 1) the spirit of fear, 2) the spirit of distraction, 3) the spirit of inconsistency, 4) the spirit of abortion, 5) the spirit of complacency, 6) the spirit of insecurity, 7) the spirit of insufficiency, and 8) the spirit of sabotage. The most important ingredient in spiritual warfare is the Word of God. The Word must be active in your daily life and daily

language in order to exercise authority over spiritual adversaries. You cannot fight a spiritual battle in your flesh. You must use the weapons that God prescribes in 2 Corinthians 10:4, which says, *"For the weapons of our warfare are not carnal, but mighty through God to the pulling down of strong holds."*

In the spirit of this verse, I have included eight of a plethora of weapons that I have used to successfully counteract my eight enemies of purpose when declared with the authority of Jesus Christ. All enemies of purpose are enemies of God, which means they are all subject to the authority of God's Word. Therefore, always use His Word in spiritual warfare.

Fear. *"For God hath not given us the spirit of fear; but of power and of love and of a sound mind."* (2 Timothy 1:7)

Distraction: *"Be sober, be vigilant; because your adversary the devil, as a roaring lion, walketh about, seeking whom he may devour."* (1 Peter 5:8)

Inconsistency: *"And he said unto me, My grace is sufficient for thee: for my strength is made perfect in weakness...."* (2 Corinthians 12:9)

Abortion: *"I shall not die, but live, and declare the works of the LORD."* (Psalm 118:17)

Complacency: *"That ye be not slothful, but followers of them who through faith and patience inherit the promises."* (Hebrews 6:12)

Insecurity: *"I can do all things through Christ which strengtheneth me."* (Philippians 4:13)

Insufficiency: *"Trust in the LORD with all thine heart; and lean not unto thine own understanding."* (Proverbs 3:5)

Sabotage: "...for the battle is not yours, but God's." (2 Chronicles 20:15)

Every other enemy of purpose not named in my list can be countered by the following "weapon of mass destruction":

> "Finally, my brethren, be strong in the Lord, and in the power of his might. Put on the whole armour of God that ye may be able to stand against the wiles of the devil. For we wrestle not against flesh and blood, but against principalities, against powers, against the rulers of the darkness of this world, against spiritual wickedness in high places. Wherefore take unto you the whole armour of God, that ye may be able to withstand in the evil day, and having done all, to stand. Stand therefore, having your loins girt about with truth, and having on the breastplate of righteousness; And your feet shod with the preparation of the gospel of peace; Above all, taking the shield of faith, wherewith ye shall be able to quench all the fiery darts of the wicked. And take the helmet of salvation, and the sword of the Spirit, which is the word of God: Praying always with all prayer and supplication in the Spirit, and watching

thereunto with all perseverance and supplication for all saints." (Ephesians 6:10-18)

I have included these weapons of warfare in the hope that you would utilize them as the foundation for your personal study on spiritual warfare. This chapter is a call to action. This book was not intended for you to read and do nothing. It was intended to propel you to respond "YES" to God's call to birth your purpose against all odds.

CHAPTER FOUR

Environment

When a woman is expected to give birth, everything and everyone inside of the delivery room must be sterile. The level of cleanliness must be conducive to what is getting ready to enter into it. The baby must be born into a clean environment. A clean environment promotes health and demotes infection. The cleaning such as mopping, sweeping and dusting are done prior to the mother's coming into the delivery room. A taboo in hospitals is to bring a patient, especially an expectant mother who is already in such a vulnerable state, into a room without performing proper hygiene on every nook and cranny of the room. Hence, housekeeping employees normally clean and re-clean the same areas multiple times a day.

Like expectant mothers, your environment must be sterilized prior to the birth of what you are carrying in your spirit. This sterilization helps to ensure that after the carrying, your "baby" is birthed in purity. You cannot afford to expose your "newborn" to impurities; after all, they could be deadly! After all of the pressure, pains and distress you endured to bring forth the "baby," do not get all the way into the delivery room and watch it take its last breath. Sterilize your environment to avoid a premature death.

EXTERNAL ENVIRONMENT

Examining every person, place and thing in your external environment becomes crucial. Your environment must be filled with those who are encouraging you into purpose—not discouraging you away from it.

Recognize that your environment is difficult to change because it is familiar to you. However, difficult does not mean impossible. Your environment is like breathing; you become so used to it that you do it without even thinking. Likewise, we entertain the same circle of friends, date the same type of people and even repeat the same mistakes simply because it all becomes a part of our normal way of life. We even accept the same things we inwardly despise because we are used to them. We rarely consider our close friends to be toxic to our well-being or the impact that our inner circle has on our view of the world around us. *People of purpose must surround themselves with like-minded individuals who are not intimidated by their greatness but have the ability to enhance it.*

Regularly performing an external inventory of who and what is around you is vital. If you detect anything or anyone with the potential to contaminate your environment, GET RID OF THEM. Yes, let them go ASAP. You will never make it to your purpose being attached to people whose mindset is beneath where God is trying to take you. If you are surrounded by people who can only affirm where you are and refuse to acknowledge where you are going, GET RID OF THEM. Like the leaves in fall change, seasons in a person's life change. Be sure that those around you are not carry-ons from an old season.

God matures those who are willing to be made mature. God will not force anyone to grow up. This means if you are growing into your purpose and your peers refuse to grow, they are a threat your growth. "*Do not be deceived: Bad company ruins good morals*" (1 Corinthians 15:33, ESV). These persons can fall into any one or more of the following categories:

> "...*lovers of their own selves, covetous, boasters, proud, blasphemers, disobedient to parents, unthankful, unholy, Without natural affection, trucebreakers, false accusers, incontinent, fierce, despisers of those that are good, Traitors, heady, high-minded, lovers of pleasures more than lovers of God; Having a form of godliness, but denying the*

*power thereof: **from such turn away.**"* (2 Timothy 3:2-5)

The Bible is clear; GET RID OF THEM. Turn away, and do not look back. God is essentially saying, "Beware of those who carry impurities that will contaminate the sterile environment He intends for your purpose to live in." These individuals will pollute the purpose of God in your life without any care or conviction because they do not care enough to walk in their own purpose. Why would they care about you walking into yours?

Motive

As you conduct your external examination of your environment, assess what each individual's intention is in your life. It does not matter how long someone has been your friend or family member because like the weather, people change and so can their motives. Even the one you think you know, who loves you like a sister or brother can be the very one who stabs you in the back.

Consider Lucifer. God created him, which means he *was* good because everything God created *was* good (Genesis 1:31, Colossians 1:16). However, when Lucifer became puffed up pride and consumed with how beautiful he was, his motive changed from leading the worship of God to desiring worship for himself. This principle still holds true today. When people possess an inflated sense of who they are, they will quickly try to deflate your sense of who you are. Satan, with an inflated sense of who he was, attempted to deflate Christ's sense of who He was by tempting him in Matthew chapter 4. Thanks be to God, Christ knew who He was, thus rendering Satan's attempt as an epic fail.

Satan's defeat at the hand of Christ shows us that when we stand in the truth of who we are, evil motives will be exposed. These motives do not have the power to alter God's purpose for your life. Do not get bent out of shape when people in your life show you who they really are. *Examine their intention but do not lose your intensity.* Go after your purpose with everything you have!

Purpose demands that people leave you. Watch out for people who try to rain on your parade, who are always negative, who always end up hurting you or speaking against what God has spoken over your life. Beware of people who are close to you when you have nothing, but as soon as

God blesses you, they are nowhere to be found.
Some will not be able to stand seeing you blessed,
so they must exit beforehand. This is to be
expected. Some people will only *see* the Promised
Land, but you, my friend, will enter in. Some will
only see the milk and smell the honey, but God will
fill your cup until it overflows.

Character

Those who walk away, talk behind your
back and secretly hope you fail are those who the
Bible refers to as "ravenous wolves who dress in
sheep's clothing" (Matthew 7:15, NASB). At one
point, they were all for what God said about you—
until it actually happened. Their jealousy,
insecurity and envy will not allow them to stick

around. Become acceptable with that kind of betrayal—even expect it. Their actions only mean that God has promoted you in the Spirit, and those who remain on your previous level have no choice but to stay there because they were not promoted, you were!

THE EXACTLY EXAMINATION

One morning while eating breakfast in a public place, I could hear four to five different conversations occurring nearly in sequence. Each one of the conversations included the word *exactly* as a reply. In fact, the word *exactly* was uttered several times before the other person even finished his or her statement. Every time I heard the word *exactly*, it stood out profoundly. Then the Lord spoke to me and said, "Purpose requires an *exactly* examination." This means that everyone with whom you surround yourself must be put to the test. An *exactly* responder simply agrees with your comment without even considering the content. I find this response problematic because it shows the person was more interested in responding than understanding.

People who lack understanding but choose to respond are not able to offer fruitful feedback. Whenever someone responds without understanding his or her response should be rejected. In John 18:10, when the chief priest and Pharisees came to arrest Jesus, Peter responded swiftly by severing the ear of Malchus, the high priest.

Jesus immediately rejected Peter's response because it lacked understanding. Peter did not take time to accurately assess the situation to gain understanding. If he had, perhaps he would have been able to realize Jesus had to be arrested in order to fulfill His purpose. However, since he was eager to respond without understanding, Jesus not only rejects his response but reiterates His purpose.

In the same way, while examining those around you, be prepared to reject responses that lack understanding because they can be detrimental to the fulfillment of your purpose. Not only must you reject uninformed responses but beware of people who *only* agree with you. People who never question or challenge you cannot add to your life.

Purpose requires your aligning yourself with those who have an understanding of who God has called you to be and will challenge you to become that person. These are the type of people who will cheer you back to the bank after your loan was declined because they believe in the business you are purposed to own. You want to avoid those who willingly attend your pity party without any attempt to drive you back into your place of purpose. Anyone who can idly stand by and watch you self-sabotage is not someone who wants you to make it to your purpose. They actually aid in keeping you away from it. Those who are aware of what God has placed on the inside of you and do not help to get it out of you are dangerous.

God would have me to tell you to consider people's words and actions toward you after a prophetic word is released over your life. Watch who speaks against what God says. Those who cannot handle your purpose will be sure to oppose it. Do not take their opposition personal; after all, they are not opposing you. They are opposing God. They did not call you to that purpose; He did. They did not anoint you for that purpose: He did. Therefore, follow the wisdom of Acts 5:39, which clearly states, *"...if it is of God, you will not be able to overthrow them; or else you may even be found fighting against God."* What a perilous place to be in! Who would want to be found standing against the Almighty God who makes one to live and another to die? Do not allow people who stand against God to deter you from purpose; rather, give them to God because they are not angry with you. They are angry with God. He knows best how to deal with them, so simply release them to Him and walk freely into all He has called you to be and do.

INTERNAL ENVIRONMENT

THE MIND

The mind is the control center of your body. All day long, your glorious mind sends signals throughout your body that produce movement, ideas, emotions and much more. Whether or not you realize or are aware of it, your mind is responsible for every decision you have ever made in your life. This small, yet complex and powerful, organ regulates all bodily activity. Simply put, it enables what you think to become what you do. That's powerful! Paying attention to what thoughts come to your mind is vital—especially the ones that take up the most mental space.

Have you ever wondered why people kill themselves? Quite simply, they could not stop the thoughts of suicide bombarding their mind. The thought consumed them so much until they attempted or unfortunately committed suicide. This morbid reality reveals exactly how powerful your mind is. Your mind has the power to control your actions whether good or bad. Your future decisions will first start as a thought before they become reality.

Ponder this question: what takes up the most space in your mind? Be honest with yourself and from these three options, choose one: God, myself or things. Obviously, no great mystery is at play here, simply Biblical truth. Romans 8:6 says, *"For to be carnally minded is death; but to be spiritually minded is life and peace."* Ever wonder why lust, sadness, despair or depression keeps being present in your mind? You are too carnally minded. The truth is, if you allow these carnal thoughts into your mind, you will die spiritually. This part of the book may make you want to walk away because it is a hard truth for anyone to confront. I promise, if you search out the matter, God will show you something life-changing.

I believe it is far easier to point out the reasons why everyone else around you is carnal, but purpose calls you to look at your own level of carnality. Let's get real. Some days are "me, myself and I" days; other days are "it's-all-about-them" days. How many days have you had this month that were "all-about-God" days? Going to church does not count. I am referring to your personal relationship with Christ. Oh, and not the public one you portray before man because at the end of the day, that means nothing. God knows your mind and what consumes it. The Bible tells us that He knows your thoughts before you do! He knows exactly who you are and what you are about. He knows if you are about His business, your business or other people's business. When you are spiritually minded, you will operate from a place of life and peace. You will not know what it is to have dead ideas or to be concerned about dead things, situations or relationships.

You can think yourself into purpose by thinking about God. The more you consume your thoughts with His Word, His truths and His instructions, the more His purpose will be revealed in your life. The less time and attention you give to idolizing yourself or others, the more time you can spend with the Lord. By spending time in the presence of the Lord, He will wash your mind, rid you of every thought contrary to your purpose and fill your mind with thoughts obedient to Christ. All He needs you to do is think about Him. Meditate on His Word.

Seriously, when is the last time you meditated on God's Word? And I am not referring to the time you memorized a new scripture. I am addressing the last time allowed His Word to take root in your spirit and become a part of your daily actions. *"For as he thinketh in his heart, so is he"* (Proverbs 23:7). When you allow the Word of God to consume your mind, you will become what it says. You do not merely preach Jesus when in a pulpit or on a street corner; your life constantly testifies of Him.

Allow Him to take up the most space in your mind—until you have no other desire than to become what He said. The opinions of others will not matter when you are consumed with Him. His voice will become magnified in your spirit so all other outside voices that do not align with His are drowned out.

This type of truth may be "too deep" for shallow people who are content where they are because they know everything. However, for you who are fed up with being bound by your own thoughts and want God to wash your mind completely, place your right hand on your head and pray this prayer:

> *Lord, let my thoughts please You. Let my mind be filled with Your truths. Let my ideas be on one accord with Your Word. Let my mind be spiritual; let it be filled with life and peace. Lord, let my mind not idolize others or things or even myself, but let my thoughts adore You alone. Grant me the desire to meditate on Your Word until it becomes a part of my daily life. Lord, let me not merely talk about You*

in public, but let me exalt You privately in my mind—in the place that no one else knows about but You. Lord, send Your anointing to my mind and destroy every yoke that causes my thoughts to be out of line with Your Word. Let Your glory consume my mind. Let this mind be in me which was also in Christ Jesus. In Jesus' name, Amen.

BODY

A person of purpose is someone who is really motivated or really lazy. If you fall into one of the two categories, it is a sure sign that God wants to birth purpose out of you.

When your body or flesh responds in a negative way, view it as a confirmation that the Spirit is saying the complete opposite. These two are in constant warfare with one another as Romans 7 so accurately captures. Therefore, one of the biggest challenges you will face is your own body! As you know, *"...the spirit indeed is willing, but the flesh is weak"* (Matthew 26:41). The flesh will never want what the Spirit wants for your life; therefore, you must cling tightly to the willingness of the Spirit.

If you are a lazy person, it will be easy for your flesh to keep you from fulfilling God's purpose for your life. Therefore, you must learn to use what works against you. Laziness is your opponent, but if you learn how to use it to your advantage, it loses its power. Gaining an awareness of your laziness is the first step to being able to overcome it. Now that you realize it, you can use that knowledge to benefit you.

How so, right? Well, if you are lazy, it is proof that you have the time to actually do something productive. If you have the time to be lazy, then finding time is not an issue for you, time management is. If you start to use your idle time to do something productive, you will see the change that you desire. I do not believe that lazy people do not want better; rather, it is the fact that they become accustomed to not doing better. They *settle* where they are.

How many times have you settled—even though you knew you deserved better? Once you get sick of settling for mediocrity, the time has come to birth purpose. Lazy people are the best candidates because all they need is a time-management plan. You need to analyze your day and note where you spend the most time. Once you see what fills your day, you can make the necessary changes.

Use Your Lazy

Where do you physically go that takes up your day? Work? The shopping mall? Or your couch of nothingness? Wherever your body is most comfortable, challenge it! That's right, challenge your body. For instance, if you are a "couch of nothingness" dweller, for the next seven days while on the couch, read a book about opening a daycare. The next week, remain on the couch and watch videos about the rules and regulations to owning your own daycare; take notes. Then, begin creating designs of the type of advertising materials you want to utilize.

As you can see, the key is to create a new normal. Get your body used to doing something different while it thinks it is doing the same ol' thing. Yes, you may be sitting on that same couch, but now you are pursuing purpose from the place where laziness once prevented you. The more you pursue, the more you will produce. Eventually, you will leave that couch and find yourself in a bank, ready to open your first business account. Use the laziness to your advantage. Fill your time with things that will lead you closer to purpose, and that purpose will manifest!

Doing Too Much

Dear Mr. or Mrs. Busybody, this section is just for you. You work, work and work while barely making time for you. You run here, there and everywhere for everybody but still have not gotten to the nail salon or massage spot you keep saying you are overdue for. The time has come for you to recognize that your busyness may not mean productiveness! On the contrary, busyness could mean procrastination. Chances are you are so busy that you do not even realize you are procrastinating. You fill every day on your calendar with something that must be done immediately. You schedule endless deadlines, you always have another meeting and when you do actually have time to breathe, you remember something else that needs to be done.

May I lovingly suggest to you that you may be unconsciously avoiding your true purpose in God by doing everything else but what He has purposed you to do. Perhaps what God gave you to do is too hard to believe so rather than going after it, you do something else. Perhaps that is why you start things and do not finish them. Perhaps that is why every time God speaks to you, rather than follow it through, you go and start another project that YOU want to do and then become discouraged when it does not work out. As one of my undergrad professors used to say, "If you ever find yourself too busy for God, you are just that—TOO busy."

Your best friend is here for you; her name is *Prioritize*. Seriously though, you need to put what God said first and foremost, and then concern yourself with everything else. God has been trying to birth His purpose in your life for a while, but you keep putting it on the back burner. The time has come for you to give God a true "Yes" and not a "Yes, right after I...."

There is a blessing in putting God first that can only be released when you obey. God will give you everything you need in this life, if you put Him first as Matthew 6:33 affirms: *"But seek ye first the kingdom of God, and his righteousness; and all these things*

shall be added unto you." You will not have to worry,

fret or become anxious about how the projects you

begin will work out—if you put Him first. It will

save you a lot of trips to the doctor, stress relievers

and even medication if you will put God first. You

cannot do everything, which is why your body tries

to.

Remember that your flesh is always saying

the opposite of your spirit. Therefore, God says,

"You need Me" while your body says "I got this."

Every time you flood your calendar with

purposeless activities and ignore what God told

you to do, you send a message to God which

confidently says, "I got this." This type of mentality

works against the purpose of God because it works

against God. Saying "I got this" is a carnal mentality, which is hostile to God.

Romans 8:7 (HCSB) says, *"For the mind-set of the flesh is hostile to God because it does not submit itself to God's law, for it is unable to do so."* Since the carnal mind will not submit to God, it can never be in agreement with the plan or purpose of God for your life. It offers you an option to do it your way, which ultimately will fail. Regardless of how successful a person may appear to be, if the success is wrought outside of the will of God, it is failure.

Take on the mind of Christ. Submit yourself, your plans, your thoughts, and your ideas completely to God. Stop doing everything in your own strength and allow the Lord to truly use you, work through you and increase in you. God has the power to exceed your greatest expectation, but He is waiting for you to get out of the way so He can.

Will you get out of His way? I would if I were you!

SOUL

Genesis 2:7 shows that after God created man from the dust of the ground and breathed life into him, man became a living soul. Man is the only created being who possesses a soul. The soul is what separates man from the rest of creation. Specifically, when we die, our souls will live on forever in eternity. Here on earth, our human souls are made up of our will, emotions, thoughts and desires. It is of the highest importance that our souls lead us toward purpose and not away from it. If you are not careful, your soul could be the very thing working against your purpose.

Consider what takes up the most emotional time in your life. When I thought about it, I realized it was someone close to me whom I often worried about. I worried because I wanted the best for this person, but they simply did not want better for themselves. I feared that this loved one's destructive life choices would one day become their demise. Countless times I have tried to help, offer advice, pray, fast and even plead with this loved one to stop making bad decisions—to no avail. I even allowed my emotions to overtake me so much so to the point that I became physically ill because I was so stressed out by my loved one's poor choices.

To make a very long story short, God instructed me to "cut the tie." I was unsuccessful on many occasions until God showed me it was a soul tie. To be clear, not all soul ties are sexual; some are emotional. Your soul can be emotionally tied to people, places or things that will work against your purpose. When God spoke "cut the tie" to me, what He meant was for me to emotionally detach my soul. I had allowed my soul to become so emotionally entangled in someone else's problems that I was no longer in tune with my purpose.

Let's stop here for a minute and consider what I have shared. Can you think of what or to whom you are so emotionally attached that is keeping you away from your purpose? If so, it's time to make the conscious decision to cut the tie!

Purpose demands a cut. While bringing forth your purpose, you will lose people and things that mean much to you. Severing ties is all a part of the process. In Matthew 4:21 and 22, Jesus calls James and John to follow Him while they were on a ship with their father Zebedee. Immediately, they left the ship and followed Him. They not only left behind the ship and their business, they also left their father. Being fishermen, they were in their place of comfort on the ship, but their purpose required them to cut the tie with their comfort zone. Are you willing to cut the tie with your comfort zone? If you are reluctant to change, then you are not ready for purpose.

Anything outside of your comfort zone introduces change. Whenever something is cut, it brings about a change. You must adjust to life without it. You must be open to the newness that life has to offer you in the absence of what has been severed. James and John had to adjust to life outside of their comfort zone and without their father, the very one from whom they had come. Other than to each other, it is very probable that James and John were next closest to their father. They had to step into their purpose without their father. In other words, purpose can cost you family members. You will have to leave behind some people and even family while in pursuit of what God has for you. Cutting ties will not be easy; it will hurt and bring weeping, but I promise for every hurt you endure, God will heal.

By gaining an awareness of what your soul has taken hold of will help you to determine whether or not it is working for or against your purpose. You will discern what promotes your freedom to walk into purpose and what prevents your moving forward. Galatians 5:1 states, "...*be not entangled again with the yoke of bondage.*" This verse is referring to the liberty Christ has given us from sin and urges us not to be associated with it again, and the same is true for emotional, mental and even spiritual matters.

It is possible to be in bondage and not even know it. I was. I had no idea that attempting to help someone out of a pit was causing me to be bound. Although I was not in a sinful type of bondage, I was in emotional bondage. My thoughts, desires and will were all fixed on helping someone who did not want to change. Be careful when you are a person of passion because sometimes you can assume others will have the same passion as you do. However, purpose calls you to deal with YOU. I had to face my own desire to fix someone who should have been given over to God long ago. I learned the lesson, albeit a hard one to learn, cut the tie and now am free to share my story with you.

Whether or not you realize it, someone needs to hear yours, but as long as you are in emotional bondage, you cannot tell it. You can be putting someone else's deliverance on hold because you refuse to cut the tie. The thing about the matter is this: if you do not do it, God will. When the Lord is ready to birth purpose through you, He will do whatever it takes—even if that means severing the tie for you!

As you cut the tie, *"Now may the God of peace Himself sanctify you entirely; and may your **spirit** and **soul** and **body** be preserved complete, without blame at the coming of our Lord Jesus Christ"* (1 Thessalonians 5:23, NASB).

CHAPTER FIVE

Innate Ingredient

Due to food shortage in the winter season, bears hibernate by curling into a ball in a den that has been prepared prior to winter and going to sleep. Bears lie torpid in the den all winter, living off their fat or stored energy. Within a few days, their body functions including the flow of blood to the heart, lungs and brain change; the heart rate drops, respiration slows down and the stomach and intestines do not function, which means the bear neither defecates or urinates. However, the bear still needs protein and water every day in order to survive. So how does the sleeping bear obtain the necessities of life? Ready for this? The bear obtains everything from within its own body, using a special form of recycling that does not exist in other animals.

The bear produces a waste product known as "nitrogen urea."[vi] For all other animals, this waste product is life-threatening because of the resulting buildup of toxicity levels. Nevertheless, the bear is the only animal to benefit from its own potentially deadly waste because the bear is able to divert the nitrogen into special pathways that generate amino acids and new proteins to enable the bear to survive. NO OTHER ANIMAL ON EARTH HAS THIS ABILITY.

Let this scientific wonder be spiritual evidence that no matter how long you have been curled into a fetal position because of the conditions you are facing, like the bear, you possess an innate ingredient that was designed to reject death and promote life – your purpose. The same God who innately implanted the ability to recycle nitrogen urea in the bear to ensure its survival during hibernation has innately implanted purpose in you. This means, you were born with it. This does not mean you should die with it. God put you here to manifest it. For this reason, He has given you everything you need to bring it forth, and 2 Peter 1:3 affirms this truth. "According as his divine power [God] hath given unto us all things that *pertain* unto life and godliness...." Therefore, everything your purpose needs to survive is already within you, waiting to be withdrawn. That is why no matter how many times you get diverted, you end up back on your journey to purpose. Even if you fall asleep (or into a human hibernation), your innate ingredient will still be producing until you "wake up."

Your innate ingredient is why you have been misunderstood and labeled as "nothing" or "nobody"—as if your purpose were dead. People do not realize what they see is not the death of your purpose; instead, it is your innate ingredient reproducing itself. Like every other animal besides the bear, purposeless people cannot produce the needed ingredient because it will literally kill them. However, God has anointed you to produce something that others would die even attempting to produce. People often speak death to your purpose because they themselves cannot carry it! Let their words be your confirmation that they can see your innate ingredient, but they simply cannot handle it. If they can see it, that means it is *still* producing; after all, your innate ingredient was created to produce.

Conclusion

When I decided to go into chaplaincy, people thought I was crazy and let me know their unsolicited thoughts, including the following: "You'll never be able to handle it because you're too young." Or "People will be biased against you because your religion is different." Or "You'll never have a career because there aren't any jobs in that field." These three statements were the most common, repetitive responses I received, but something inside of me kept saying, "You were created for this!"

After being accepted into the program and completing my CPE internship in August of 2015, no jobs were available in the hospital where I completed my internship. Although I was a bit discouraged because I loved where I was and those with whom I worked, I kept applying, searching and even traveling out of state to find a chaplain position. In January of 2016, I unexpectedly received three calls nearly simultaneously for three different interviews. After attending all three interviews, I was offered all three positions! Hallelujah! I began to seek God for direction as to which open door I should walk through. Within a week, I received another call, but this time from the hospital in which I had interned, offering me a position that did not exist—but had been created just for me! I knew this offer was of GOD!

I was moved to tears of joy as I accepted the position with thanksgiving. I could not thank God enough for the devout leaders who saw the innate ingredient God had placed within me and allowed me to exercise my gifts in such a prestigious hospital. I must also add that right when I thought God had finished blessing me, about a year later another position was created for me. This position offered me double what I was making, full benefits, leadership responsibilities and my own office! Never mind "Cry Me a River"! I cried an ocean of gratitude to God and the virtuous leaders who believed in me. Please let my story serve as proof that despite all of the odds you will initially face while endeavoring to birth purpose, I can promise IT WILL HAPPEN because you were born to produce it!

God is saying to you this day, "Do not give up now! You were created for this! You were built for this! You will withstand the storm! You will defy the odds! Your purpose will live, thrive and survive." My friend, you have something that no one else in the world had or will ever have—a tailor-made purpose given to you before the foundation of the world. Therefore, when it looks like there is a lack, a drought or a shortage in what you need to birth purpose, know this: IT'S ALREADY IN YOU! Everything you need has already been imparted into your spirit by the Creator. Every idea, strategy and resource is already in you. What's more, as a believer, the same Spirit that raised Christ Jesus from the dead now lives in you. My friend, you have *every* answer you will ever need. When you received Jesus into your heart as your personal Lord and Savior, you received the Spirit of a survivor! Jesus was not only born to die but He was born to live again! His purpose required death to bring forth life. My brothers and sisters, there will be some days you may feel like your purpose has died but let the spirit of Christ in you reassure you that what once was dead will live again! He could not stay dead because His purpose called Him to life! I decree over every reader, your purpose has been called to life! It will live and not die to declare the work of the Lord! You will not just walk in it but you will soar in it against all odds! On your journey, may the Spirit of Christ teach, enrich, edify and empower you!

If you have not already received Jesus as your personal Lord and Savior, the following is expressly for you:

The Bible declares in John 3:16, *"For God so loved the world, that he gave his only begotten Son, that whosoever believeth in him should not perish, but have everlasting life."* God loves you so much, my friend, that He wanted to make sure that when you die, you will live with Him forever in Heaven. So He sent His Son, Jesus Christ, to pay the debt you owed, I owed, and every other human being who ever lived owed.

The Bible says in Romans 6:23, *"For the wages of sin is death; but the gift of God is eternal life through Jesus Christ our Lord."* The first part of this verse means every bad thing that you do here on earth adds up to death—an *eternal* death, meaning when you die, you will go to Hell. The good news is that Jesus didn't conclude the passage at this point. The second part of the verse says that you do not have to go to Hell because God is offering you the gift of eternal life, which means you will go to Heaven. Accepting that gift is very easy; all you have to do is take it—like you accept someone's gift at Christmas or a birthday celebration. If you believe that Jesus died for your sins and rose again on the third day with all power and authority in His hands, the Bible says you are saved. Being saved means you are free from having to pay any penalty for the sins you have committed; instead, you will live eternally with Christ in Heaven.

If you believe in your heart that Jesus died for your sins, say this prayer:

Lord Jesus, I believe You died for me and
rose again. I repent of my sins and receive
You now as my Lord and Savior. Come into
my heart and make me Your child. In Jesus'
name, Amen.

CONGRATULATIONS! IF YOU BELIEVE THIS
PRAYER YOU PRAYED, YOU ARE NOW SAVED!
Find a local, Bible-believing Christian church to
assemble with others and grow deeper in God's
Word! May the Lord bless you!

———————————

About the Author

Daphne R. Beard is a full-time professional Interfaith Chaplain in a Level II Trauma Center hospital in New York where she offers spiritual and emotional support to persons of all faiths. Daphne is certain that her calling is not limited to a specific people group but fervently believes the anointing of God surpasses all racial, religious and gender boundaries. Her areas of specialty include but are not limited to death and dying, trauma, crisis and grief.

After being licensed to preach the Gospel in December of 2013 and ordained in August of 2016, Daphne is humbled to serve as Elder of the Outreach Ministry in a local Baptist Church where she leads a team that offers free meals, clothing and Christ to the less fortunate.

Daphne received her Bachelor of Arts Degree in Biblical and Theological Studies from Nyack College in Manhattan, New York and her Master of Divinity Degree in Chaplaincy from Liberty University in Lynchburg, Virginia. To GOD be all the glory!

Acknowledgments

To the best mother in the world, you have exemplified what it means to overcome against all odds and achieve success. You have showed me how to survive in the worst of times and rejoice in the best of times. Thank you for always believing in me and encouraging me in everything I do. You have been there every step of the way on this project but more importantly in my life and I am forever grateful to you for all you have done and continue to do. I love you more than words can express!

To my brother and sister, thank you for your continued love, support and tolerance of my late night typing sessions while finishing this project. As you grow up, I pray that you often refer back to Gods word and this God-given manuscript to help you overcome life's challenges. You guys make me so proud and I love you both.

To the greatest spiritual parents, Pastors and covering a girl could ask for, Bishop and First Lady Jason C. McCants of the Cathedral at New Gethsemane Baptist Church East and West Campuses in New York. You have seen in me what I did not see in myself. Your passion for excellence has pushed me to more fervently strive to be all that God has called me to be. Thank you for the ongoing love, genuine support and countless impartations. Love you both!

To the most gracious editor, Linda Stubblefield of Christian of Affordable Christian Editing in Merrillville, IN. Your decades of editing experience and teaching in seminary are evident in your work on this project. Thank you for words of wisdom and carrying everything out with the spirit of excellence.

To the most patient graphic designer, Jorge Hagans of Resido Designs in Richmond, VA. Thank you for tolerating my perfectionist ways and never showing any signs that I got on your nerves. From on-going, tedious changes to a number of redo's – you took my feedback, maintained an incredible turnaround time and truly brought my vision to life.

To the most encouraging photographer, Melvin Garrett of MelGFilms in Long Island, NY. Thank you for capturing the most important moments. From start to finish, you understood the heart of this project and worked to bring it to fruition with great precision.

To the Cross Carriers Publishing team, words are not enough to express my gratitude!

Endnotes

[i] "Why Non-Smokers Sometimes Get Lung Cancer, 1 November 2016, American Cancer Society, http://www.cancer.org/cancer/news/features/why-lung-cancer-strikes-nonsmokers. Accessed 10 April 2017.

[ii] Collins English Dictionary (Pocket edition) Tenth Edition. "Languages Direct. Accessed June 10, 2017. https://www.languages-direct.com/collins-english-dictionary-tenth-edition.html.

[iii] Strong, J. (1996). *The new Strongs exhaustive Concordance of the Bible: with main concordance, appendix to the main concordance, topical index to the Bible, dictionary of the Hebrew Bible, dictionary of the Greek Testament. Nashville: T. Nelson.*

[iv] Soukhanov, Anne H. *Microsoft Encarta Dictionary. New York, NY; St. Martins Paperbacks, 2004.*

[v] Strong, J. (1996). *The new Strongs exhaustive Concordance of the Bible: with main concordance, appendix to the main concordance, topical index to the Bible, dictionary of the Hebrew Bible, dictionary of the Greek Testament. Nashville: T. Nelson*

[vi] Ibid.

[vii] Mammal anatomy: an illustrated guide. New York Marshall Cavendish, 2010.

46329595R00094

Made in the USA
Middletown, DE
29 July 2017